PASS YOUR
GCSE MATHS
Shape and Symmetry

Dear Student,

Thank you for buying this book. It will help you with your GCSE Maths by showing you how to gain extra marks. Just one of those marks could move you up a grade. Remember that there is only one mark difference between a Grade D and a Grade C.

Most of the double page spreads in the book consist of three sections: 'What You Need to Know', 'Revision Facts' and 'Questions'.

Read 'What You Need to Know' carefully, making sure that it makes sense to you. You may find it helpful to work with someone else so that you can check that each other understands.

Use the 'Revision Facts' as a reminder - you may like to copy these into an exercise book to create a revision guide to use nearer to your exam.

Try all the 'Questions', even those that are easy but especially those that appear to be difficult. There is an answer section in the centre that you can pull out so that you can check your work. If you find that you have made a mistake, don't worry but just try to see where you went wrong. You can learn a lot from mistakes.

To answer some of the questions you may need a ruler, a pair of compasses, a protractor or a calculator. Make sure that you have all of these ready and in good working order.

You will find other aspects of shape work in our books 'Angles and Triangles' and 'Measures', both in the Pass Your GCSE Maths series.

Good luck,

Andrew Brodie

WHAT YOU NEED TO KNOW

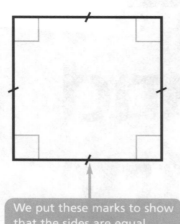

A square has 4 equal sides and 4 right angles.

We put these marks to show that the sides are equal.

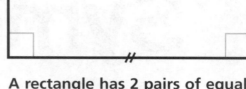

A rectangle has 2 pairs of equal sides and 4 right angles.

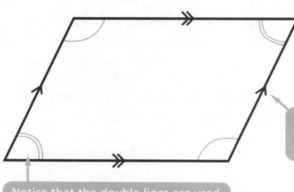

A parallelogram has 2 pairs of equal sides and 2 pairs of equal angles. The angles add up to 360°.

The single arrow is used to show that <u>this</u> side is parallel to the other side with a single arrow.

Notice that the double lines are used to show that <u>this</u> angle is equal to the other angle with double lines.

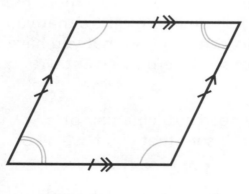

A rhombus has 4 equal sides (like a square) and 2 pairs of equal angles (like a parallelogram). The angles add up to 360° (like all quadrilaterals).

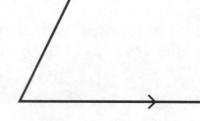

A trapezium has one pair of parallel sides.

REVISION FACTS

✓ All four sided shapes are called quadrilaterals.

✓ The only **regular** quadrilateral is a square, because all its sides are equal and all its angles are equal.

✓ The interior angles of a quadrilateral always add up to 360°.

QUESTIONS

Calculate the sizes of the missing angles on each of these quadrilaterals.

Note: The diagrams are not drawn accurately because the examiner doesn't want you to measure them.

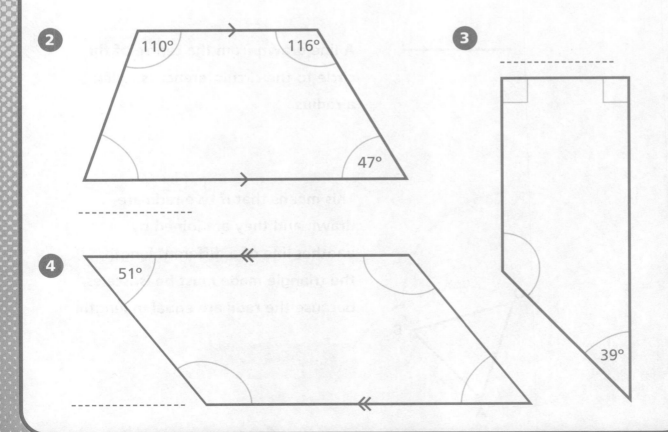

❶ 91° 84° 63°

❷ 110° 116° 47°

❸

❹ 51° 39°

WHAT YOU NEED TO KNOW

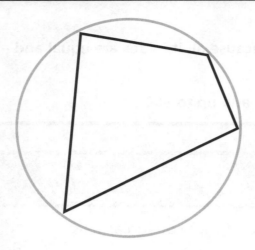

A quadrilateral drawn inside a circle is called a cyclic quadrilateral. (Provided all its corners touch the circumference.)

The opposite angles of a cyclic quadrilateral add up to 180°.

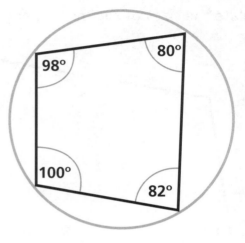

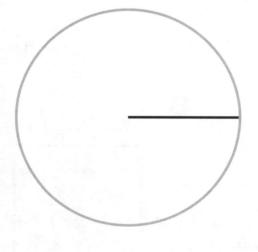

A line drawn from the centre of the circle to the circumference is called a radius.

This means that if two radii are drawn and they are joined by another line of a different length, the triangle made **must** be isosceles, because the radii are equal in length.

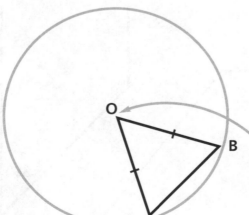

The centre of the circle is often given the letter O.

REVISION FACTS

✓ A quadrilateral drawn so that its corners touch the circumference of a circle is called a cyclic quadrilateral.

✓ The opposite angles of a cyclic quadrilateral add up to 180°.

QUESTIONS

Find the missing angles in these quadrilaterals.

1

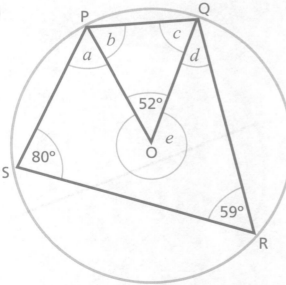

We write this angle like this: ∠ ABC

The middle letter is the letter of the point.

We write this angle: ∠ BCD

∠ DAB = _____

∠ ABC = _____

2

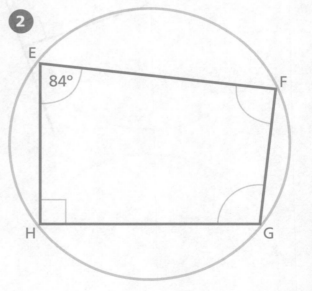

∠ EFG = _____

∠ FGH = _____

3

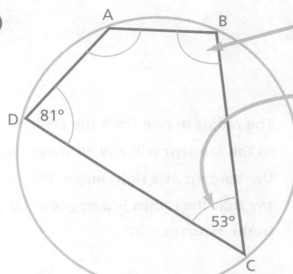

Tip: Use your knowledge about isosceles triangles to help you with this one.

Tip: Work out the sizes of *b* and *c* first.

∠ *a* = _____

∠ *b* = _____

∠ *c* = _____

∠ *d* = _____

∠ *e* = _____

WHAT YOU NEED TO KNOW

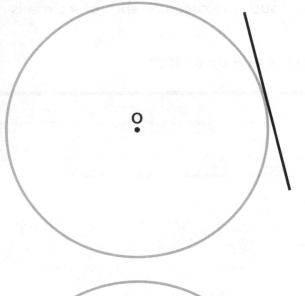

A line that just touches a circle is called a **tangent**.

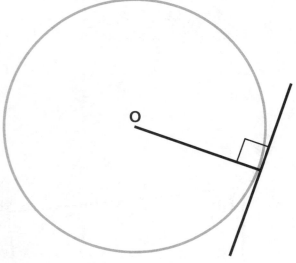

The radius drawn from the centre to the tangent will always meet the tangent at a right angle. We say that the radius is **perpendicular** to the tangent.

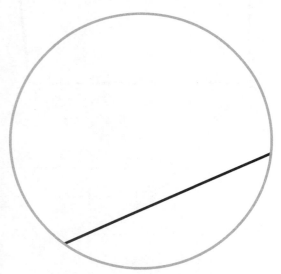

A line that joins two points on a circle is called a **chord**.

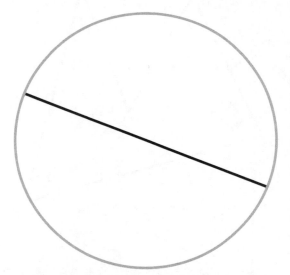

A chord that passes through the centre is called a **diameter**. A diameter is equal in length to two radii.

REVISION FACTS

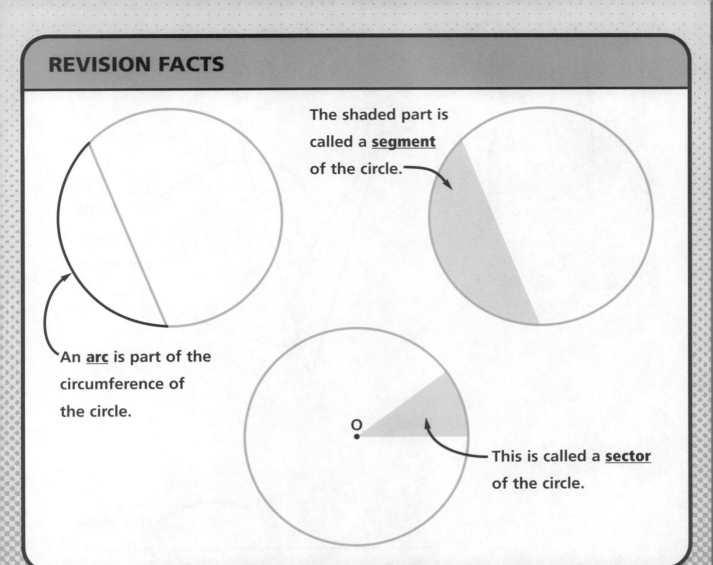

The shaded part is called a **segment** of the circle.

An **arc** is part of the circumference of the circle.

This is called a **sector** of the circle.

QUESTIONS

Label the circles.

This curved line is an _____

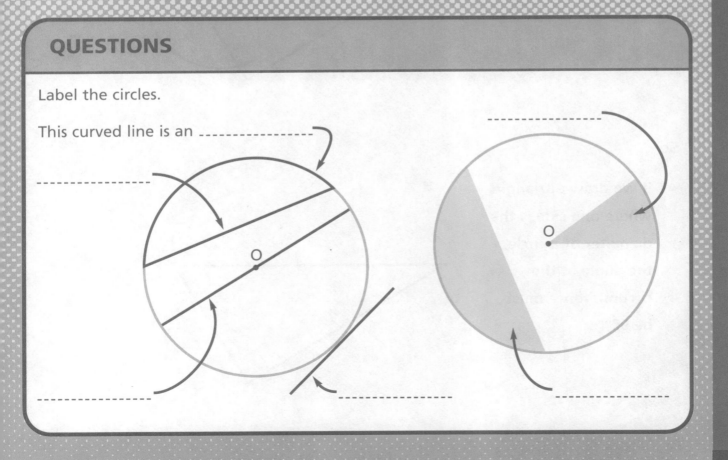

WHAT YOU NEED TO KNOW

Tip: The angle subtended by an arc at the centre of a circle is double the angle subtended by the same arc at the circumference.

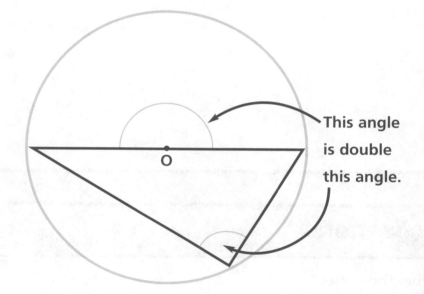

This angle is double the size of this angle.

So ...

This angle is double this angle.

So ...

If we draw a triangle where one side is the diameter of a circle, the angle at the circumference must be 90°.

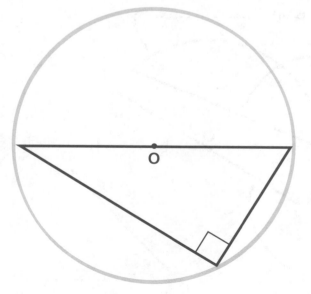

REVISION FACTS

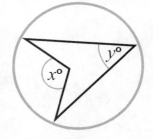

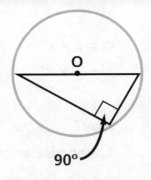

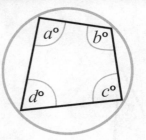

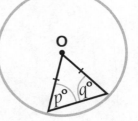

$x° = 2 \times y°$

(so $y° = \frac{1}{2} \times x°$)

90°

$a° + c° = 180°$

$b° + d° = 180°$

$p° = q°$

QUESTIONS

Find the sizes of all the marked angles.

Remember: The diagrams are not to scale so you can't measure the angles.

1

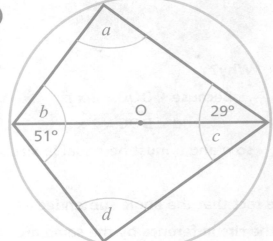

a = _____

b = _____

c = _____

d = _____

Tip: You may not be able to find the answers in this order.

2

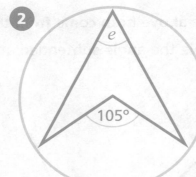

105°

e = _____

3

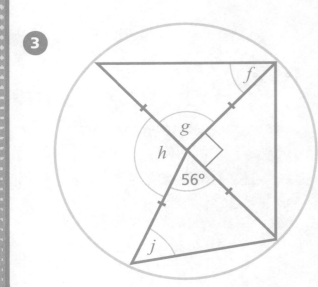

f = _____

g = _____

h = _____

j = _____

Tip: It's easier to do these in a different order.

WHAT YOU NEED TO KNOW

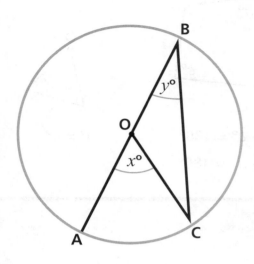

$x° = 2 \times y°$

$y° = \frac{1}{2} \times x°$

Why?

... Because angle y is subtended at the circumference by the arc AC

... and angle x is subtended at the centre by the arc AC. (Just like the first revision fact on page 9.)

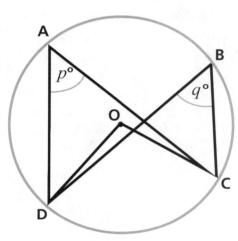

$p° = q°$

Tip: Angles in the same segment are equal.

Why?

... Because $\angle$ DOC = 2 x p

... and $\angle$ DOC = 2 x q

so p and q must be equal in size.

The two examples above both come from the fact that the angle subtended at the centre is double the angle subtended at the circumference by the same arc. Here is a new fact:

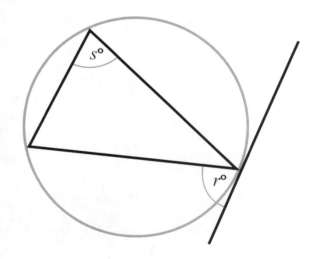

$r° = s°$

Tip: The angle subtended at the circumference by a chord is equal to the angle made between the chord and a tangent.

REVISION FACTS

✓ Angles in the same segment are equal.

✓ The angle subtended at the circumference by a chord is equal to the angle made between the chord and a tangent.

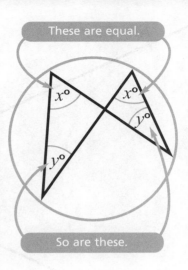

These are equal.

So are these.

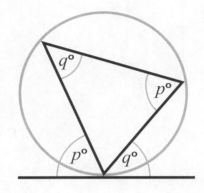

QUESTIONS

Find the sizes of the marked angles.

1

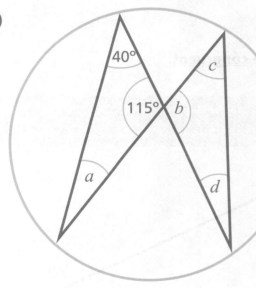

a = _____

b = _____

c = _____

d = _____

> Remember, they don't have to be done in this order.

2

e = _____

f = _____

g = _____

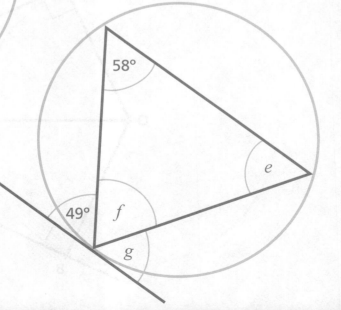

WHAT YOU NEED TO KNOW

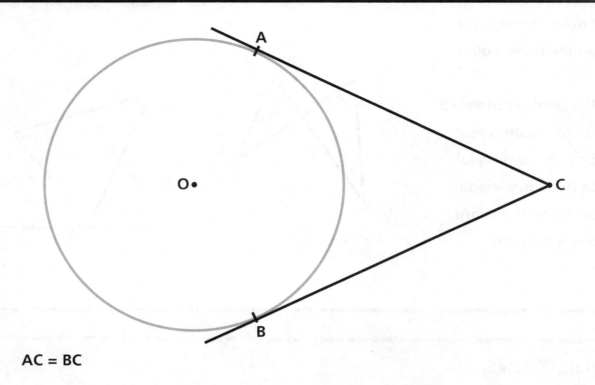

AC = BC

The line AC is equal in length to the line BC because tangents from the same point are equal.

This means that the triangles AOC and BOC are **<u>congruent</u>**.

> Tip: Congruent triangles are triangles with equal size angles and equal size sides.

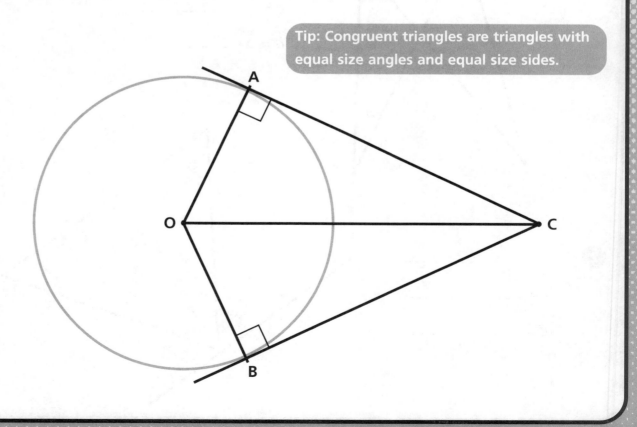

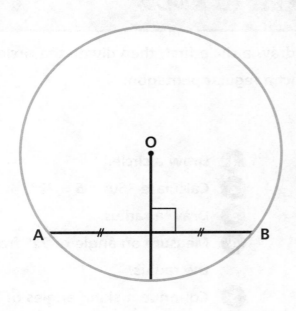

A radius that crosses a chord at right angles, cuts the chord in half. We say that this radius is the perpendicular bisector of the chord.

A bisector cuts something in half.

Perpendicular means at right angles.

REVISION FACTS

✓ Tangents from the same point are equal.
✓ The perpendicular bisector of a chord is a radius.

QUESTIONS

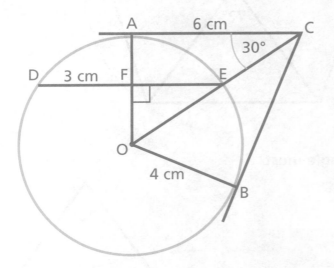

Find:

∠ OCB = _____

∠ OBC = _____

∠ BOC = _____

Find these lengths:

FE = _____

BC = _____

OE = _____

OC = _____

OF = _____

Tip: You will need to use Pythagoras for two parts.

WHAT YOU NEED TO KNOW

One way to draw a regular polygon is to draw a circle first, then divide the circle into equal angles. For example, to construct a regular pentagon:

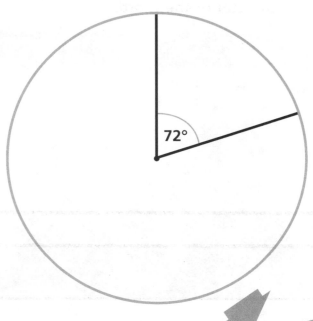

1 Draw a circle.

2 Calculate 360° ÷ 5 = 72°

3 Draw a radius.

4 Measure an angle of 72° from the radius.

5 Continue making angles of 72°

6 Join the points around the circle.

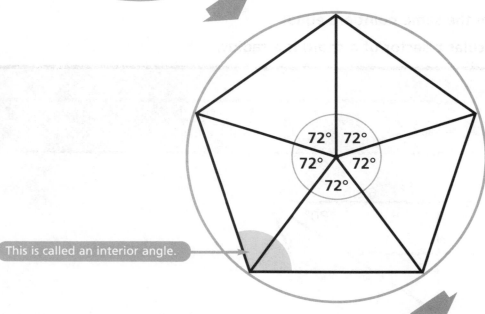

This is called an interior angle.

You can see that the interior angle must be 108°, because 54° + 54° = 108°

These angles must be 54° because 72 + 54 + 54 = 180

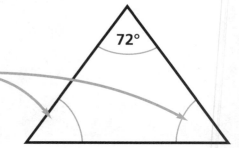

ANSWERS

p3.　**1** 122°　　**2** 87°　　**3** 141°

4

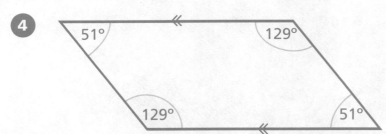

p5.　**1** ∠ DAB = 127° (180° − 53°)　　∠ ABC = 99° (180° − 81°)

2 ∠ EFG = 90°　　　　　　∠ FGH = 96°

3

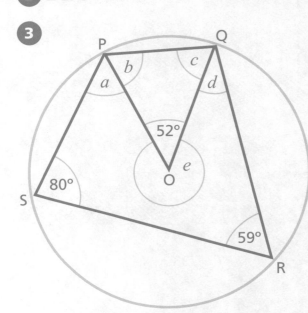

To find b and c:
　Because triangle OPQ is isosceles
　　　　　∠b = ∠c
　$b + c + 52° = 180°$
　　so $b + c = 128°$
　　　so $b = 64°$ and $c = 64°$

To find a:
　∠SPQ + 59° = 180°
　(opposite angles of cyclic
　quadrilateral) so ∠SPQ = 121°
　$a = 121° − 64° = 57°$

∠$a = 57°$　∠$b = 64°$　∠$c = 64°$
∠$d = 36°$　∠$e = 308°$

p7.

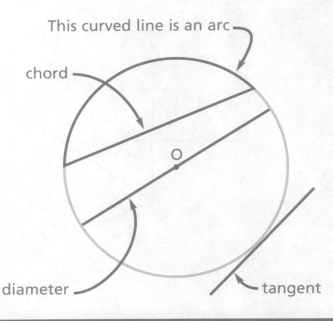

This curved line is an arc

chord

diameter

tangent

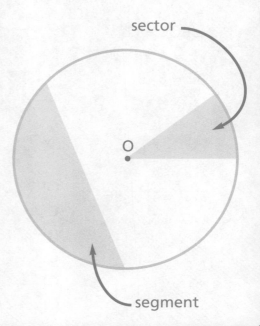

sector

segment

p9. **1** $a = 90°$ Because it's in a triangle where one side passes through the centre.

$90° + 29° = 119°$ so $b = 61°$

$d = 90°$ $90° + 51° = 141°$ so $c = 39°$

2 $e = \frac{1}{2} \times 105° = 52.5°$

3

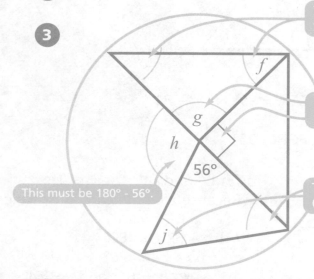

These two must be equal because they are in an isosceles triangle.

This must be 90° because this one is 90°.

Do this one first.

$f = 45°$

$g = 90°$

This must be 180° - 56°.

These two must be equal. (Isosceles triangle).

$h = 124°$

$j = 62°$

p11. **1** $a = 25°$ Because the other two angles of the triangle add up to 155° so $a = 180° - 155°$.

$b = 115°$ Opposite angles where two straight lines cross.

$c = 40°$ Because angles in the same segment are equal.

$d = 25°$ Because angles in the same segment are equal.

2 $e = 49°$ $\qquad g = 58°$ $\qquad f = 73°$

p13. $\angle OCB = 30°$ Because it's the same as $\angle OCA$.

$\angle OBC = 90°$ Because it's where a radius meets a tangent.

$\angle BOC = 60°$ Because $90° + 30° = 120°$ and $180° - 120° = 60°$.

$FE = 3$ cm Because the line OA is a radius crossing the chord DE so it must be bisecting it.

$BC = 6$ cm Because it matches AC.

$OE = 4$ cm Because it is a radius.

$OC^2 = OB^2 + BC^2$ (pythagoras)

$OC^2 = 4^2 + 6^2$

$OC^2 = 16 + 36$

$OC^2 = 52$

$OC = \sqrt{52}$

$OC = 7.2$ cm

$OF^2 = OE^2 - FE^2$

$OF^2 = 4^2 - 3^2$

$OF^2 = 16 - 9$

$OF^2 = 7$

$OF = \sqrt{7}$

$OF = 2.6$ cm

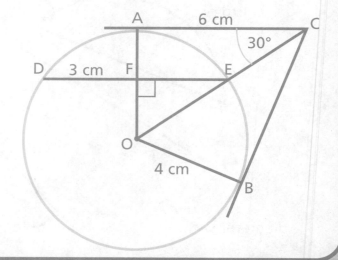

ANSWERS

p19.

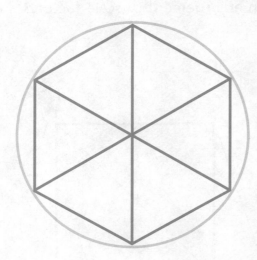

To draw a regular hexagon the angle at the centre must be 60° (360 ÷ 6).

Now look at one of the triangles. If the angle at the centre is 60° the other two must add up to 120° (180 – 60).

Because they are equal:
120 ÷ 2 = 60°
so each interior angle = 120°.

p21. a = 76°. To find this you had to work out the sum of the interior angles = 180° x 3 = 540°, then subtract the angles that were already shown.

   b = 104° c = 62° d = 60° e = 63° f = 71°

p23.   **1** The square has 4 lines of symmetry and rotational symmetry of order 4.

   2 The shape is a hexagon. It has 3 lines of symmetry and rotational symmetry of order 3.

p25.   Shape A has been reflected in the line $x = {}^-2$ to form its image B.

p27.   Shape A has had a rotation, through 90°, anti-clockwise, about the point (2,2).

p29.   Shape J maps on to shape J' by a translation of 10 squares to the right and 5 squares down. This is a translation of $\begin{pmatrix} 10 \\ -5 \end{pmatrix}$.

p31. Shape A maps on to shape B by an enlargement of scale factor 3 and centre (2,1). Look:

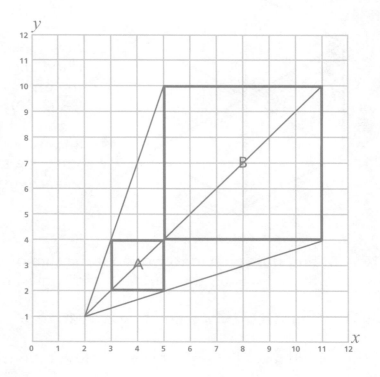

p32. Shape A has a height of 3 squares so the enlargement will have a height of 12 squares.

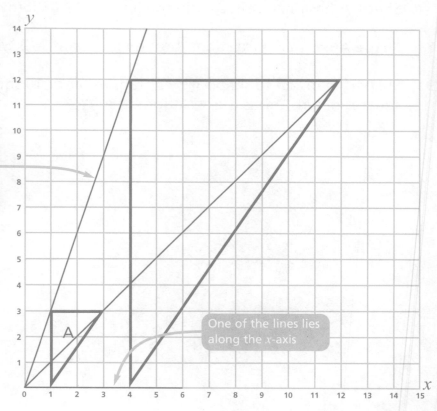

Draw these lines accurately so that they lead from the origin and pass exactly through the corners of Shape A.

One of the lines lies along the x-axis

WHAT YOU NEED TO KNOW

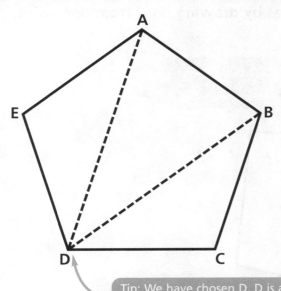

Another way find the size of the interior angle of a regular polygon is like this:

1 Choose one point.

2 Draw lines from that point to those that it's not already joined to - this makes three triangles.

3 Each triangle has 180° so the total of the interior angles is 180° x 3 = 540°.

4 Each interior angle = 540° ÷ 5 = 108°.

Tip: We have chosen D. D is already joined to E and C, so join it to A and B. This makes three triangles.

REVISION FACTS

✓ Regular polygons can be drawn inside circles by dividing 360° by the number of sides then drawing lines at the resulting angle from the centre.

✓ Find the total of interior angles by splitting the polygon into triangles. Each triangle has 180°.

QUESTION

Draw a regular hexagon, then find the size of one of the interior angles.

Tip: Interior angles are **not** the angles at the centre of the circle, just the ones at the corners of the hexagon.

WHAT YOU NEED TO KNOW

Irregular polygons can also be split into triangles by drawing lines from one point.

Look:

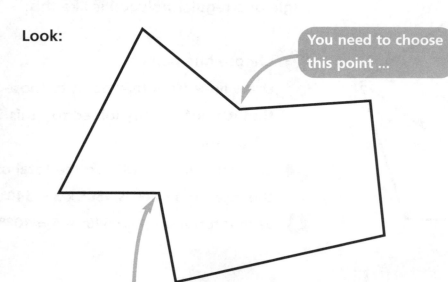

You need to choose this point ...

... or this point, because you can't reach all the other corners from the other points.

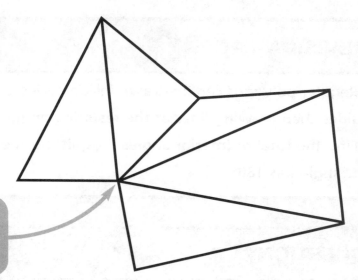

You can see that we have drawn four lines from this point to split the shape into 5 triangles.

The shape is a seven sided shape called a heptagon. The sum of the interior angles of the heptagon is 5 x 180° = 900°. We can't work out the size of each angle because the shape is irregular so they are not all the same.

Tips:

5 sided shapes can be split into 3 triangles.

6 sided shapes can be split into 4 triangles.

7 sided shapes can be split into 5 triangles.

You can see that the number of triangles is 2 less than the number of sides.

Exterior angles are formed by extending the sides of the shape.

For **this** shape, each exterior angle = 180° − 120° = 60°.

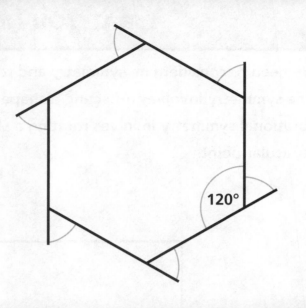

120°

REVISION FACTS

✓ To find the sum of the interior angles of a polygon, subtract 2 from the number of sides then multiply by 180°.

✓ To find the exterior angles, extend each side then subtract the interior angle from 180°.

QUESTIONS

Find the sizes of the angles indicated.

Diagram not drawn accurately

a = ...

b = ...

c = ...

d = ...

e = ...

f = ...

d 120°

c

118°

117°

e

109°

f

a *b*

WHAT YOU NEED TO KNOW

We need to consider line symmetry and rotational symmetry.

Line symmetry involves reflecting a shape or a picture using a mirror line.

Rotational symmetry involves rotating a shape or a picture around a particular point.

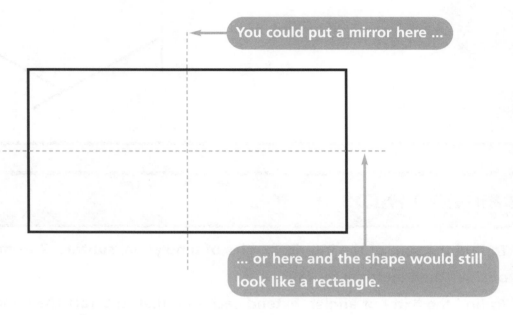

You could put a mirror here ...

... or here and the shape would still look like a rectangle.

A rectangle has two lines of symmetry.

A rectangle also has rotational symmetry.

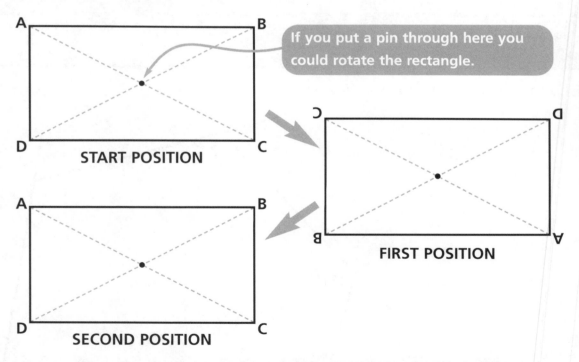

If you put a pin through here you could rotate the rectangle.

START POSITION

FIRST POSITION

SECOND POSITION

You can see that the second position is the same as the start position.

We say that the rectangle has rotational symmetry of order 2.

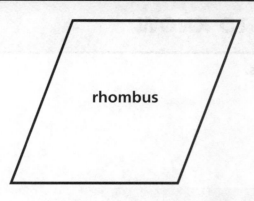

rhombus

A rhombus has 2 lines of symmetry and it has rotational symmetry of order 2.

A parallelogram has **no** lines of symmetry. If you put a mirror on it, the shape would not be a parallelogram. Try it!

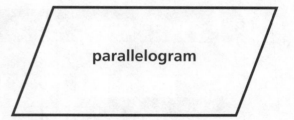

parallelogram

… but it does have rotational symmetry of order 2.

REVISION FACTS

✓ A shape has line symmetry if a mirror could be placed on a line so that what is visible looks like the original shape.

✓ A shape has rotational symmetry if it can be rotated to fit over its original position.

✓ The order of rotational symmetry is the number of times a shape can be rotated to its original position.

QUESTIONS

How many lines of symmetry do these shapes have?
What order of rotational symmetry do they have?

1

Shape: _____

Lines: _____

Order: _____

2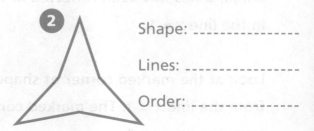

Shape: _____

Lines: _____

Order: _____

WHAT YOU NEED TO KNOW

We can apply various transformations to shapes.

We often use grid paper for this work.

One type of transformation is a reflection.

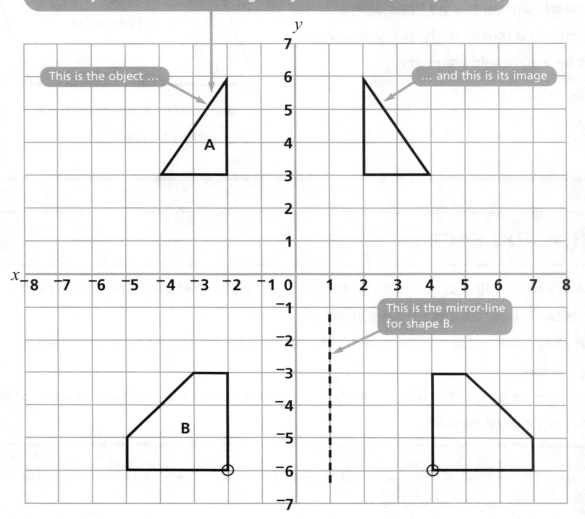

If the object is called A the image may be called A' (we say: A dash)

This is the object ...

... and this is its image

This is the mirror-line for shape B.

You can see that shape A has been reflected in the y axis (where $x = 0$).

Shape B has not been reflected in the y axis. Shape B has been reflected in the line $x = 1$.

Look at the marked corner of shape B - it is three squares from the line $x = 1$. The marked corner of its image is also three squares from the line $x = 1$.

REVISION FACT

✓ To find the line of reflection, choose one point on the object, find how far it is to the matching point on the image then go halfway between them. Check you are right with one of the other points.

QUESTION

This is how a GCSE question might be worded:

Describe the single transformation that maps shape A on to shape B.

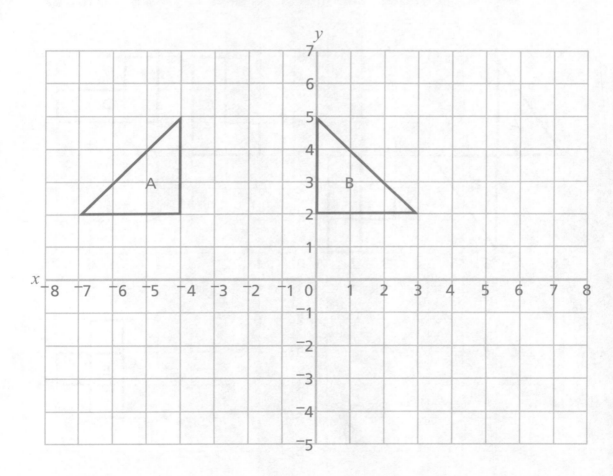

You can see that this transformation is a reflection so you must say that in your description and you must identify the mirror-line.

WHAT YOU NEED TO KNOW

Another type of transformation is a rotation.

When describing a rotation you need to give four bits of information:

1 The shape has had a transformation by **rotation**.

2 The rotation is through an angle of …°.

3 … clockwise or anticlockwise?

4 The rotation is about the point (… , …).

Look at these three examples.

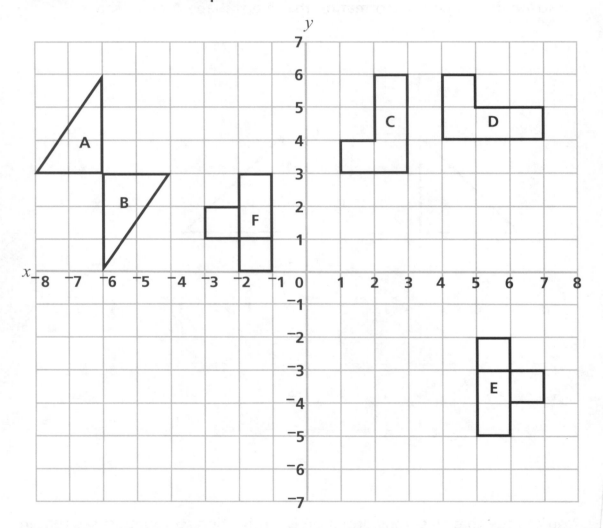

Shape A has been mapped on to shape B by a rotation through 180° clockwise about the point (⁻6, 3).

Shape C has been mapped on to shape D by a rotation through 90° clockwise about the point (4, 3).

Shape E has been mapped on to shape F by a rotation through 180° anticlockwise about the point (2, ⁻1).

The easiest way to find the centre of rotation (the point about which the object has been rotated) is to trace the object using tracing paper or very thin paper. You can then hold the tracing paper with the tip of a pencil, trying different points while you rotate the paper. This will also help you to find the angle of rotation.

REVISION FACTS

Transformation by rotation needs to be described in four ways:

1 rotation   **2** angle of ...°   **3** clockwise or anticlockwise?

4 about the point (... , ...)

QUESTION

Describe the single transformation that maps shape A on to shape B.

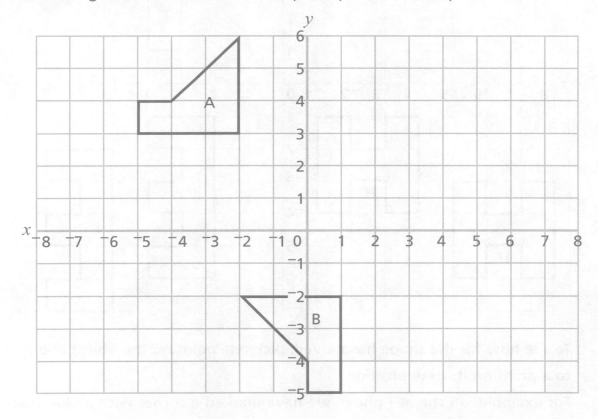

WHAT YOU NEED TO KNOW

When describing a translation you need to give three bits of information:

1 This is a translation.

2 How far left or right the shape has moved - in other words, how far it has moved in the x direction.

3 How far up or down the shape has moved - in other words, how far it has moved in the y direction.

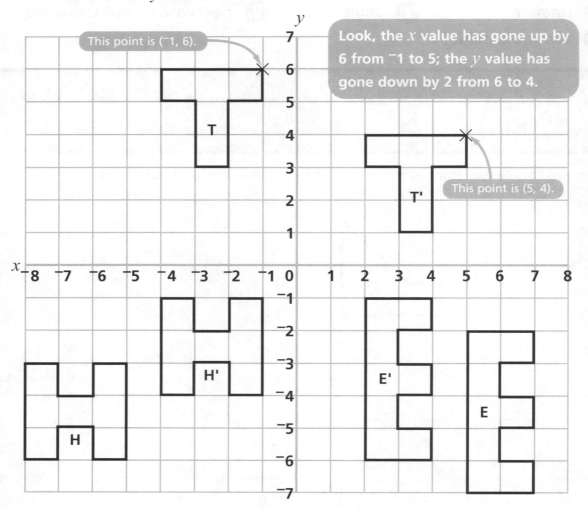

This point is ($^-$1, 6).

Look, the x value has gone up by 6 from $^-$1 to 5; the y value has gone down by 2 from 6 to 4.

This point is (5, 4).

To see how far the shape has moved, pick one point on the object and match it to a point on its new position.

For example, on shape T above we have marked a corner with a blue cross.

How far has the cross moved in the x direction to get to T'?

It has moved 6 squares to the right.

How far has the cross moved in the y direction?

It has moved 2 squares down.

We can show the translation of shape T to shape T' as a **column vector**:

$\begin{pmatrix} 6 \\ {}^{-}2 \end{pmatrix}$ ← This is the x part: up 6
← This is the y part: down 2

Let's describe the transformation that maps shape E on to shape E':

Shape E maps on to shape E' by a translation of 3 squares to the left and 1 square up. This is a translation of $\begin{pmatrix} {}^{-}3 \\ 1 \end{pmatrix}$.

The transformation of shape H on to shape H':

Shape H maps on to shape H' by a translation of 4 squares to the right and 2 squares up. This is a translation of $\begin{pmatrix} 4 \\ 2 \end{pmatrix}$.

REVISION FACTS

✓ A **translation** must be described in terms of movement left or right **and** up or down.

✓ A column vector shows the change in the x value and the change in the y value.

QUESTION

Describe the single transformation that maps shape J on to shape J'.

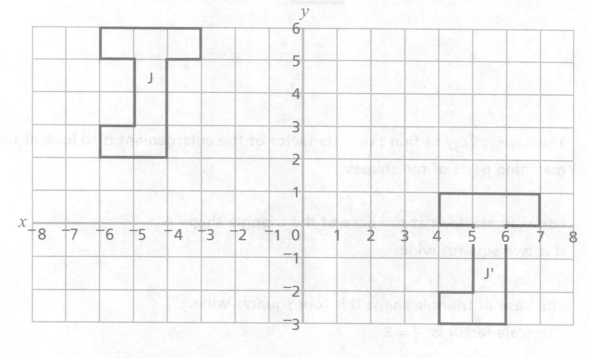

WHAT YOU NEED TO KNOW

When describing an enlargement you need to give three bits of information:

1 This is an enlargement.

2 The **scale factor** of the enlargement. (This means how much bigger, or even possibly smaller, the new shape is.)

3 The centre of enlargement.

Look:

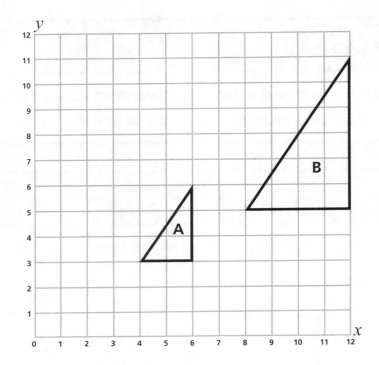

The easiest way to find the scale factor of the enlargement is to look at two matching parts of the shapes.

For example, look at the base of the triangle shape A.
It is two squares wide.

The base of triangle shape B is four squares wide.
The scale factor is $\frac{4}{2} = 2$.

The easiest way to find the centre of enlargement is to join the matching points, extending the joining lines until they meet.

Look at the diagram from page 30.

The lines meet at the point (0, 1) so the centre of enlargement is (0, 1).

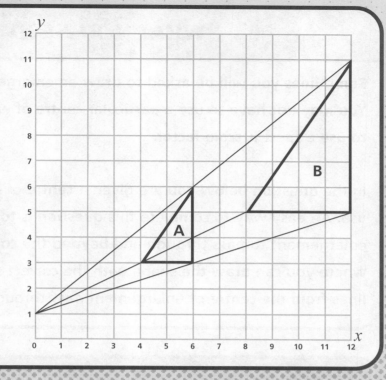

REVISION FACT

✓ Enlargements should be described in terms of **scale factor** and **centre of enlargement**.

QUESTION

Describe the single transformation that maps shape A on to shape B.

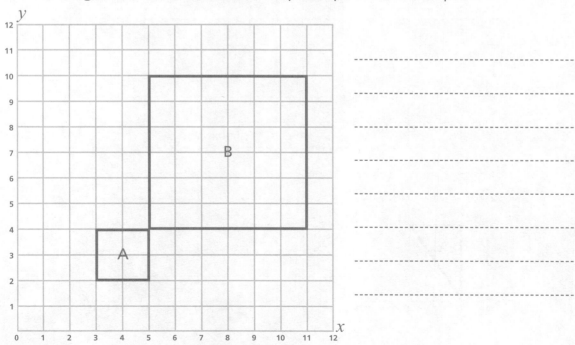

WHAT YOU NEED TO KNOW

Sometimes you will be asked to draw an enlargement.

You may not have to use a particular centre of enlargement but you will be asked to use a specific scale factor.

In the question below you are given a centre of enlargement and a scale factor to use. An easy way to complete this question is to draw lines from the centre of enlargement to pass through and beyond the corners of the shape. Then find where you can draw the shape with the correct scale factor making sure that the lines from the centre of enlargement pass through the corners of the new shape.

QUESTION

Draw an enlargement of shape A with a scale factor of 4 and centre of enlargement (0, 0). ◄—— Sometimes called the origin.

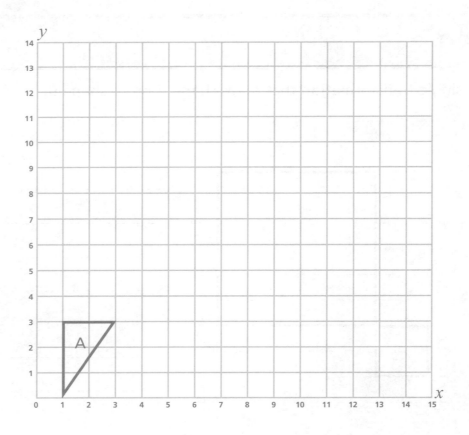